MA

Bridges

NEW EDITION

Chris Oxlade

H www.heinemann.co.uk/library
Visit our website to find out more information about Heinemann Library books.

To order:
☎ Phone 44 (0) 1865 888066
🗎 Send a fax to 44 (0) 1865 314091
🖥 Visit the Heinemann Bookshop at www.heinemann.co.uk/library to browse our catalogue and order online.

First published in Great Britain by Heinemann Library, Halley Court, Jordan Hill, Oxford OX2 8EJ, part of Harcourt Education.
Heinemann is a registered trademark of Harcourt Education Ltd.

Editorial: Diyan Leake
Design: Celia Floyd and Richard Parker (2nd ed.)
Illustrations: Barry Atkinson
Picture research (2nd ed.): Erica Newbery
Origination: Modern Age
Printed by WKT Company Ltd in China

ISBN 978 0 431 00085 5 (hardback)   ISBN 978 0 431 00092 3 (paperback)
ISBN 0 431 00085 9 (hardback)   ISBN 0 431 00092 1 (paperback)
10 09 08 07 06   11 10 09 08 07
10 9 8 7 6 5 4 3 2 1   10 9 8 7 6 5 4 3 2 1

British Library Cataloguing in Publication Data
Oxlade, Chris
    Bridges. – 2nd ed. – (Building amazing structures)
    1. Bridges – Design and construction – Juvenile literature
    I. Title
    624.2

Acknowledgements
The publishers would like to thank the following for permission to reproduce photographs: Associated Press p. 26 (Chiaki Tsukumo); Collections pp. 14 (Brian Shuel), 20 (Richard Davis), 21, 24, 25; Corbis p. 28; Eye Ubiquitous pp. 6 (Jonas Grau), 7 (Paul Thompson), 9 (Judyth Platt), 11 (Michael George), 17 (David Cumming), 18 (Kevin Wilton), 23 (John Wender); Hutchison Library p. 12; Robert Harding p. 5; Sund & Baelt p. 29; Tony Stone p. 4; Taylor Woodrow p. 16.

Cover photograph of Oresund Bridge, Copenhagen, Denmark reproduced with permission of Lonely Planet Images (Anders Blomqvist).

Every effort has been made to contact copyright holders of any material reproduced in this book. Any omissions will be rectified in subsequent printings if notice is given to the publishers.

Contents

Words appearing in the text in bold, **like this**, are explained in the Glossary.

About bridges

We take bridges for granted, but think about how tricky travelling by car or train would be without them. A bridge is a structure that supports vehicles and people as they cross over an obstacle, such as a road, railway or river. It holds up their weight and carries it down into the ground at either end of the bridge.

A structure is a thing that resists a push or pull. Many of the world's most amazing structures are bridges – tall, spindly bridges carrying trains hundreds of metres above **gorges**, and slender, graceful bridges sweeping across wide **estuaries**. But you also cross hundreds of smaller bridges, which you might not even notice as you speed along in a car or train.

What different types of bridge are there? Who decides where to build them and why? What special materials and machinery are needed?

The Golden Gate Bridge, in San Francisco, USA, was completed in 1937. The distance between the two towers is 1,280 metres (4,200 feet).

At 48.8 metres (160 feet) wide, Australia's Sydney Harbour Bridge is the world's widest bridge.

Why do we build bridges?

The main reason for building a bridge is to save time and make transport more efficient. A long bridge across a river estuary saves a trip on a ferry, or going inland to where the river is narrower. Bridges also allow railways and fast roads to remain level so trains and vehicles can keep up their speed. Bridges at road and railway cross-overs improve safety and reduce jams by avoiding busy junctions.

Types of bridge

Different types of bridge are suitable for different situations, and there are four main types. They are **beam bridges**, **arch bridges**, **suspension bridges** and **cable-stay bridges**. The type used normally depends on the **span** (the distance the bridge must stretch without a support).

FACTS ✛ Bridge world records
- Longest bridge span
  Akashi Kaikyo suspension bridge, Japan. Length: 1,991 metres (6,530 feet) – that's nearly 2 kilometres (1.25 miles) without a support! Completed: 1998
- Longest bridge overall
  Second Lake Pontchartrain Causeway, Louisiana, USA. Length: 38.4 km. Completed: 1969
- Highest bridge
  Royal Gorge Bridge, Colorado, USA. Height: a dizzying 321 metres (1,053 feet) above river level – the Chrysler Building in New York could nearly fit under it! Completed: 1929.

Bridges in the past

Many thousands of years ago, people made simple log bridges across streams. But the oldest bridges that still survive today are called clapper bridges. They are made of stone slabs supported at their ends by piles of stones. The word "clapper" comes from the Latin word *claprerius*, meaning "pile of stones".

Using the arch

The first long bridges were made of logs joined together to make **beams**, supported on stone **piers**. Long-lasting bridges had to be made of stone, but long stone beams are so heavy that they snap under their own weight. The solution to this problem was the stone arch. Ancient Rome's brilliant **engineers** became experts at building semi-circular stone arches. Their designs were so good that many of their bridges are still in use today, 2000 years after they were built.

The Pont du Gard, France, is still standing more than 2,000 years after Roman engineers built it.

The Romans also developed simple concrete, which they used in their piers, and the **cofferdam**, which helped them to build piers in the middle of rivers.

Iron and steel

By the beginning of the 19th century, engineers around the world had worked out how to make long, low stone arches and had built many graceful river bridges. They began using iron for bridge building because iron is stronger than wood and stone. Engineers started designing **arch bridges** made of iron bars and beams, and **suspension bridges** which used iron cables for support. Iron bridges had longer **spans** and were much stronger than the older stone bridges. They were perfect for carrying heavy railway locomotives over rivers and **gorges**.

Although **steel** is made mostly of iron, it is far stronger than iron alone. Steel took over as the main bridge-building material by the end of the 19th century. It started a new era of bridge building, during which engineers created gigantic **beam bridges** and arch bridges, and staggering suspension bridges.

Simple bridges

The simplest type of bridge is just a **beam** supported at each end. A good example is a tree trunk resting on each bank of a stream. The simplest **beam bridge** is a single-**span** bridge, made up of a beam supported by **abutments**. A **cantilever** is a beam supported firmly at just one end. The longer a beam is, the stronger it needs to be, and the heavier it becomes. Beam bridges do not work for spans of more than a few hundred metres because the beams would collapse under their own weight.

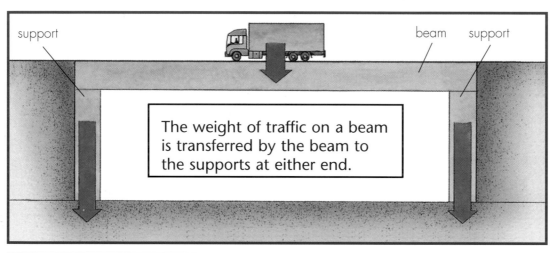

support   beam   support

The weight of traffic on a beam
is transferred by the beam to
the supports at either end.

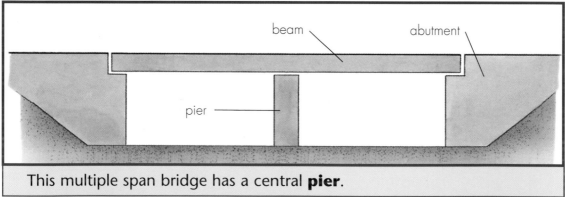

beam   abutment

pier

This multiple span bridge has a central **pier**.

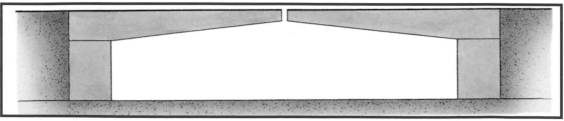

The cantilever bridge has two cantilevers, supported at one end.

Beams, girders and trusses

Keep an eye out for different types of beams. Most are made from solid **reinforced concrete**. **Girders** are made from **steel** plates **welded** together. A **truss** is made by joining together lengths of steel into a framework. A truss can be longer than a girder because it weighs less. One of the first box-girder bridges was the Britannia Bridge in Wales, completed in 1850. Trains actually travelled inside the rectangular girders.

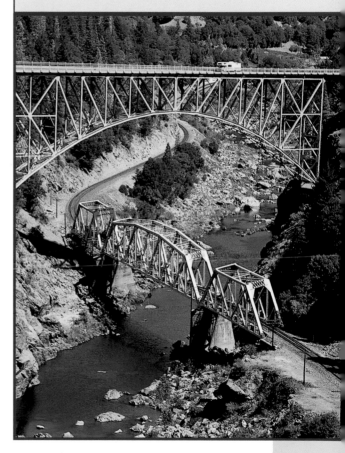

These are two truss bridges in California, USA. The top bridge is a truss arch.

Here are four different kinds of beam.

concrete beam

plate girder (steel)

box girder (concrete)

truss (steel)

TRY THIS

Bending beams

Make a simple beam bridge by supporting a large sponge at each end with books. Press down in the centre of the sponge. Can you see that the top part of the sponge is squashed and the bottom part is stretched? The squashed part is in **compression** and the stretched part is in **tension**. This iswhat happens in a real beam, but a real beam bends much less.

More bridges

Apart from the various types of **beam bridges**, there are three other types of bridge. They are the **arch bridge**, the **suspension bridge**, and the **cable-stay bridge**.

Curving arches

An arch bridge is supported by a structure that curves upwards between supports at its ends. The weight of the traffic on the bridge is carried around the arch to its ends. Because of its shape, the arch is only in **compression** – the materials in it are squashed together. There is no **tension**, or pulling apart, at all. This is why arches can be built with stone or brick, which are strong in compression but weak in tension. The ends of the arch push downwards and outwards on its **abutments**, which need to be very strong to stop the ends of the arch spreading. The biggest arches are massive **steel truss** arches, over 500 metres (1,640 feet) long and as high as a 60-storey building.

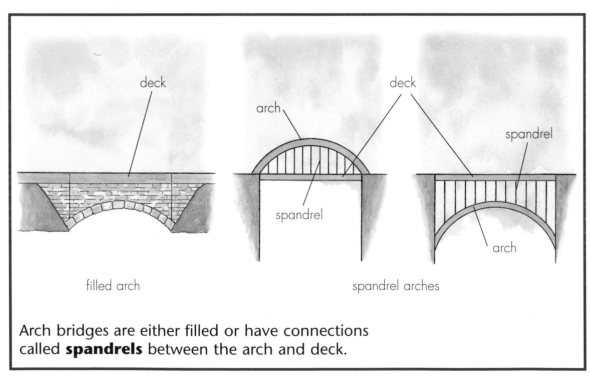

deck

arch

deck

spandrel

spandrel

arch

filled arch

spandrel arches

Arch bridges are either filled or have connections called **spandrels** between the arch and deck.

Hanging from cables

Suspension bridges are the giants of the bridge world, with **spans** of 1 kilometre (0.6 mile) or more.

Heavy anchors needed to hold the suspension cables can be seen clearly on the Verrazano Narrows Bridge in New York, USA.

The world's longest suspension bridge has a main central span of 1,991 metres (6,530 feet). It takes 20 minutes to walk from one support tower to the other! The **deck** that the traffic travels on is suspended on steel cables (called **hangers**) that are hung across the river or **gorge**. The cables are supported by tall towers, often as high as skyscrapers. The weight of the traffic goes up the hangers, along the cables, down the towers, and also into heavy ground anchors.

Cable-stay bridges

Cable-stay bridges are similar to suspension bridges. The deck is held up by cables attached directly to the towers. Cable-stay bridges can have very long spans, but not as long as suspension bridge spans.

Suspended by grass

Simple suspension bridges are made with ropes or wires hung between the banks of rivers. The ropes form handrails, and a simple walkway hangs under them. Before steel cables became easily available, the ropes were made of grass woven together.

Bridge parts

The various types of bridge look different, but they all have **piers** and **foundations**, which attach bridges to the ground, and **expansion joints** that allow the parts of a bridge to move slightly. All bridges also have a **deck** along which the traffic moves.

Piers and foundations

A pier is a support that is part way along a bridge. Some piers are made of a single square or circular column. For wide bridges, each pier may be made of two columns with a **beam** across their tops. Piers can be just a few metres high on bridges over roads or more than 100 metres (330 feet) high on bridges that go over deep valleys. Some bridges have dozens or even hundreds of piers.

Piers and **abutments** always rest on top of foundations. Foundations carry the huge **loads** of the traffic and hold the bridge itself safely into solid ground, so they often need to be very deep. They stop the bridge sinking or toppling over.

This **cable-stay bridge** has a tower (or pylon) and a pier (right). The road deck is supported by cables.

Allowing for movement

As traffic rolls across a bridge, the parts of the bridge move slightly. For example, in **beam bridges**, the beams sag a tiny bit. Changes of temperature also cause movements. The parts of a bridge **contract** slightly when the temperature falls. They **expand** again when it warms up. A **steel girder** 50 metres (165 feet) long grows about a centimetre (0.4 inch) when the temperature rises from freezing to 20 °C (68 °F).

Engineers must allow these movements to happen. If they didn't, unwanted forces are set up that could eventually break parts of the bridge. Beams rest on **bearing plates** that let the beams move and twist. Gaps are left at the ends of beams to allow for expansion. The gaps are filled with special expansion joints that stop water leaking into the gaps.

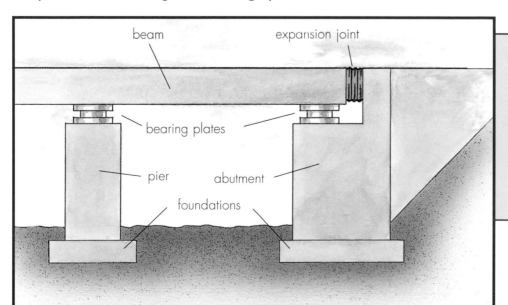

beam

expansion joint

bearing plates

pier

abutment

foundations

The diagram shows bearing plates and an expansion joint on a beam bridge.

Bridge materials

Wood and stone are useful for making small bridges because they are easy to find and use. But most large bridges today are made from concrete and **steel**.

Steel bridge beams are **prefabricated** from steel plates.

Super-strong steel

Steel is used on its own for **girders**, **trusses** and arches, often by **welding** flat steel plates together. It is also used to make cables, **hangers** and towers for **suspension bridges** and **cable-stay bridges**. Steel is immensely strong in both **tension** and **compression**. For example, a steel cable as thick as your finger could lift a 30-tonne truck.

Pouring concrete

Concrete is another important construction material. It is made up of **cement**, water and aggregate, which consists of sand and gravel or stone chips. When the ingredients are first mixed, the mixture is runny. When the cement dries and hardens, it binds the sand and gravel together.

Concrete is an excellent construction material because it is quite cheap and immensely strong. In fact, a mug-sized piece of concrete could support a 30-tonne truck. It can be set into shapes by pouring it into moulds when it is still liquid.

Reinforcing concrete

Concrete is extremely strong in compression. However, in tension it cracks quite easil, so where part of a concrete structure will be stretched, steel is added. This material, made up of concrete and steel bars, is called **reinforced concrete**.

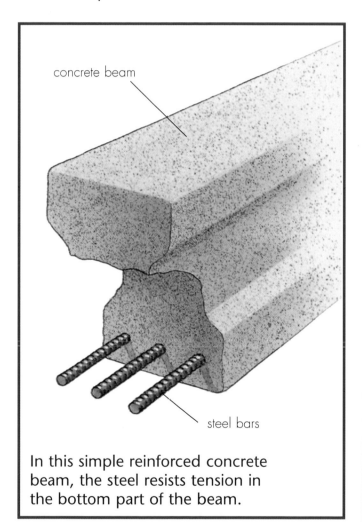

concrete beam

steel bars

In this simple reinforced concrete beam, the steel resists tension in the bottom part of the beam.

Future bridges

It is unlikely that any completely new types of bridge will be developed, but new materials may be used. Extremely long suspension bridges, with **spans** of several kilometres, are difficult to build with steel and concrete because of the huge weight. Lighter, stronger materials such as **carbon fibre** and **kevlar** might be used for the **deck** and cables.

Very long concrete **beams** are made with **pre-stressed concrete**. This means that the steel bars in the beam are stretched slightly until the concrete hardens. When they are released, this compresses the concrete, giving it extra strength. Pre-stressed concrete beams can be made thinner and lighter than normal reinforced concrete beams.

Designing a bridge

Before any construction work can begin on a large public bridge, an organization, such as a government transport department, decides that a bridge is needed. A **consulting engineer** oversees the design and construction of the bridge for the organization.

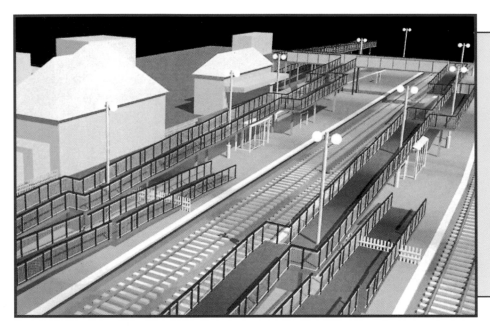

New bridges, such as this railway footbridge, are designed on a computer so that people can see what the bridge will look like before it is built.

What sort of bridge?

The type of bridge depends on its location and how it will be used. Where possible, **beam bridges** with short **beams** and lots of **piers** are chosen because they are easy and cheap to build. But if the water or valley is very deep, piers are difficult to build, so a **cantilever** or **cable-stay** bridge is the better choice.

Exploring underground

Geological investigations are made to decide what sort of **foundations** will be needed and to discover any weaknesses in the ground. Rock and soil samples are dug from **boreholes** and tested to see how strong they are.

Designing parts

Next, the **engineers** decide how strong the bridge needs to be. They calculate the maximum weight of traffic that is likely to be on the bridge at one time. This is called live **load**. The engineers add this to the weight of the bridge itself, which is called the dead load. They try to keep the dead load as small as possible, to save money and materials, without making the bridge weak.

Against the wind

The sites of long-**span** bridges are often in wide valleys, or near coasts, where the wind can be extremely strong. Bridges must be designed to resist the force of the wind, otherwise they could collapse. Sometimes they have collapsed! Engineers normally design a bridge to withstand the strongest wind that is likely to happen. In some parts of the world, this can be more than 250 kilometres (155 miles) per hour.

Footbridges often have interesting designs. This one in Uttar Pradesh, India, has cables at each side to prevent it from swaying.

Site preparation

Building a large bridge, such as a **cable-stay bridge** across an **estuary**, is an enormous operation that can take more than five years. Normally one **engineering** company, called the main contractor, is in charge of the whole construction project. Dozens of smaller companies, called sub-contractors, do special jobs such as building cables or **foundations**.

Foundations first

The first stage in building a bridge is to dig holes for the foundations. Powerful earth-moving machines do most of the work. Foundations spread the weight of the bridge and the traffic on it into the ground. The type of foundation chosen depends on what the ground is like. Slab foundations are like rafts that sit on deep, soft ground. **Pile** foundations are used to reach down through shallow soft ground to solid **bedrock**.

Pier foundations are constructed inside a cofferdam for the Second Severn Crossing between England and Wales.

Cofferdams and caissons

In water, bridge **piers** rest on heavy concrete bases. There are two ways of building these bases. In shallow water, a temporary circular dam called a **cofferdam** is built in the river. The water is pumped out and the soft, **silt** river bed is dug away until firm ground is found. Then concrete is poured in to make the base. In deep water, the bases are built using **caissons**. A caisson is a **steel** or concrete box with an open base which is dropped to the river bed. Silt is dug out from inside and the caisson sinks until it reaches firm ground. Then it is filled with concrete.

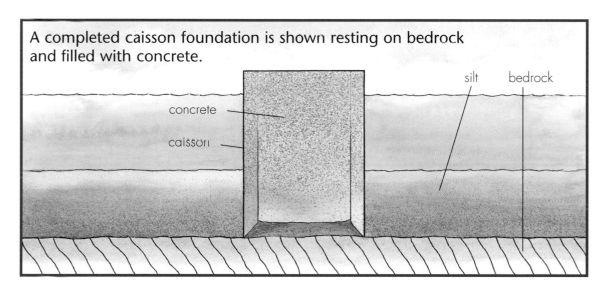

A completed caisson foundation is shown resting on bedrock and filled with concrete.

TRY THIS

Caissons under pressure

In deep water, **pneumatic** caissons are often used to keep the water from leaking in. Try this experiment to see how they work. Cover the bottom of an empty plastic tub with a layer of sand and fill the tub with water. Cut the base from a small plastic bottle. Place the bottle on the sand and blow gently into the neck. The water will flow out, leaving the sand dry.

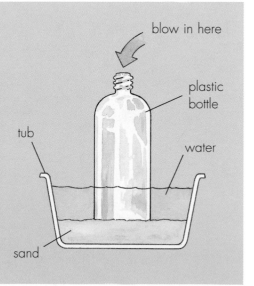

Building a beam bridge

Here you can see how a **beam bridge** is built. The first job is to dig holes for **foundations**, and, if necessary, build **embankments** which take the road at either end of the bridge up to the level of the road **deck**.

Slab foundations

Before any concrete for the foundations is mixed, a mould must be made for it to be poured into. The mould is made with wooden sheets or **steel** plates, called formwork, supported by scaffolding. The reinforcing steel is also put in place so that it will be encased when the concrete sets. The formwork stays in place until the concrete is set.

Piers and beams

Once the concrete in the foundations is set, **piers** and **abutments** are added. These are built in place using more formwork. Short piers are made in one go. Tall piers are made in stages. Concrete is poured into the formwork and is allowed to set. Then the formwork is moved up and more concrete is poured and allowed to set. This continues until the pier reaches its full height.

Reinforced concrete piers are seen here under construction. The right-hand piers have steel formwork in place.

An enormous prefabricated steel beam is lifted into place on a motorway bridge.

Bearing plates are placed on the abutments and piers. **Prefabricated** steel **beams** or **pre-cast**, **pre-stressed** concrete beams are lifted into place. Each **span** is made up of several beams side by side. Formwork is built along the sides, and concrete for the road deck poured. For very short spans a few metres long, concrete beams and slabs are built *in situ*, or on the spot, using formwork. Finally, **expansion joints** are installed.

TRY THIS
Post-tensioned beams
Long beams are often made from prefabricated hollow sections placed end to end and tightened together with steel cables. This is called post-tensioning. Find three small boxes or blocks of wood the same size. Place them end to end to make a beam. Press inwards on each end of the beam to post-tension it. Can you see how the **tension** makes the beam stronger?

Building more bridges

Cable-stay bridges and **suspension bridges** are normally built across wide rivers or between islands, with towers standing in the water.

Foundations and towers

The first stage is to build the **foundations** at the base of each tower using **cofferdams** or **caissons**. The concrete towers are often built by a method called slip-casting. The formwork for the tower gradually creeps upwards. Concrete is poured in the top of the formwork and sets by the time it reaches the bottom.

Suspension cables

Suspension-bridge cables can be more than 1 metre (3 feet) thick. They are made on site by putting hundreds of thin strands of wire next to each other and squashing them together to make the cable. The ends of the cables are connected to heavy ground anchors.

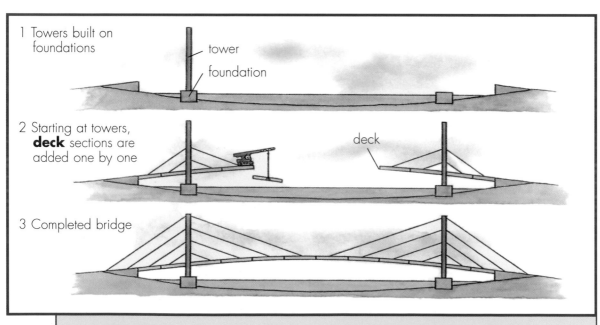

1 Towers built on foundations

tower

foundation

2 Starting at towers, **deck** sections are added one by one

deck

3 Completed bridge

This shows the stages in the building of a cable-stay bridge.

The final section of a cable-stay bridge is dropped into place. A cable will be added to support it.

Adding the deck

Each **prefabricated** section is floated into the river on a barge, lifted into place by a crane and attached to the suspension cable or tower by a **hanger** or cable. Work normally starts at the towers and progresses outwards to the sides and middle. Each new section is connected to the previous one. On cable-stay bridges, the concrete sections are pulled together with tight **steel** cables. On suspension bridges, the steel sections are **welded** together.

FACTS ✤ That's amazing!
- The Brooklyn Bridge, a suspension bridge in New York, contains 23,000 kilometres (14,300 miles) of wire in its cables. That's enough to stretch more than halfway round the world!
- The **cantilevers** of Scotland's Forth Railway Bridge are made up of 50,000 tonnes (55,000 tons) of steel tubes and **girders**.
- The suspension towers at opposite ends of the Humber Bridge in England are 4 centimetres (1.5 inches) further apart at the top than the bottom, to allow for the curving surface of the Earth!

Bridges in use

Once the structure of a bridge is complete, the bridge is prepared for use. The tarmac road surface is laid on top of the road **deck** and road markings painted on it. Safety fencing is put up along the sides of the bridge to stop vehicles skidding off in an accident. Lighting illuminates the road surface at night. Navigation lights are also added to **piers** in water for ships to spot, and to the top of towers for aircraft.

Many large road bridges are toll bridges, which drivers have to pay to cross. The tolls help to pay for the construction and maintenance of the bridge. Often a row of toll booths is built at one end of the bridge, where drivers can pay their toll without getting out of their vehicles.

London's famous Tower Bridge is a lifting or "bascule" bridge. Every so often, traffic stops so that the bridge can open to allow tall ships to pass underneath.

Bridge maintenance

A bridge needs to be maintained properly. **Steel** bridges are painted regularly to protect them from being damaged by air and water. Concrete and steel parts must be checked for cracks. Cracks in concrete can let water reach the reinforcing steel inside. Tiny cracks in steel can spread, weakening the bridge. Older bridges often need to be strengthened to stop them collapsing under the weight of heavy modern trucks.

In bad weather

Bridges are designed to stand up to high winds, but the winds can be dangerous for the traffic on them. When it is windy, speed limits slow vehicles down. High-sided vehicles, such as buses and caravans, may not be allowed to cross in case a gust flips them over! In very strong winds the bridge may be closed completely.

Instant bridges

Rivers are major obstacles for armies, especially when permanent bridges are destroyed. So army **engineers** build temporary bridges called Bailey bridges after their inventor, Sir Donald Bailey. Some come in parts which must be assembled. Others unfold from the back of special vehicles.

This Bailey bridge carries a road over a stream that has washed away the original bridge.

Bridge disasters

Modern bridges are designed to withstand heavy traffic, bad weather, floods and earthquakes. But bridges cannot stand up to unexpected events. They can be destroyed in flash floods and big earthquakes. The worst disasters happened in the past, before **engineers** fully understood structures and the materials they were using. Things can also go wrong as a bridge is built. Small mistakes in the design or unexpected rocks under the ground can delay building and increase the cost of the finished bridge.

This Japanese expressway toppled sideways during the 1995 earthquake in Kobe, Japan. The piers did not have enough reinforcing **steel** to be able to withstand the quake.

Collapse on the Tay

The Tay Bridge in Scotland, built in the 1870s, was an iron **truss** supported on dozens of tall iron **piers**. On a stormy night in December 1879, the central section of the bridge collapsed into the River Tay as a train crossed. Seventy-five passengers died. The poor-quality, brittle iron had cracked because of the sideways force of the wind on the trusses.

Bridge twister

The most famous bridge collapse happened at Tacoma Narrows in Washington state, USA, in 1940. A new **suspension bridge** had just been completed, designed to withstand winds of more than 200 kilometres (125 miles) per hour. In a wind of just 75 kilometres (47 miles) per hour, the **deck** began to move wildly up and down and twist from side to side. Eventually it broke up and fell into the river below. Fortunately no one was killed or injured. Engineers realized that the deck was not stiff enough, and the wind had been just the right speed to make it vibrate. Decks on similar bridges were quickly stiffened.

Building problems

In the past, safety on building sites was not as good as it is now. Many workers died during the construction of bridges. The worst place to work was in **pneumatic caissons**, such as the ones used to build the **foundations** of the Brooklyn Bridge (1869–1883). Many workers suffered from a condition known as the "bends" because of the sudden reduction in air pressure as they came out of the caissons. At the time nobody understood what caused the bends. Hundreds of workers were crippled, and three died.

Bridge facts

FACTS ✢ Longest spans – suspension bridges

BRIDGE	METRES	FEET	COMPLETED
Akashi Kaikyo, Japan	1,991	6,530	1998
Great Belt Link, Denmark	1,624	5,330	1997
Runyang, China	1,490	4,888	2005
Humber, England	1,410	4,625	1981
Jiangyin, China	1,385	4,544	1999
Tsing Ma, Hong Kong, China	1,377	4,518	1977

FACTS ✢ Longest spans of each type of bridge

TYPE	BRIDGE	METRES	FEET	COMPLETED
Arch	New River Gorge	518	1,700	1977
Beam	Rio Niteroi, Brazil	300	985	1974
Cable-stay	Tatara, Japan	890	2,920	1999
Cantilever	Pont de Quebec, Canada	549	1,800	1917
Suspension	Akashi Kaikyo, Japan	1,991	6,530	1998

The Akashi Kaikyo Bridge is the longest bridge in the world. Its towers are 283 metres (928 feet) high.

This bridge near Millau in France opened in 2005. It is the world's tallest, with its main tower stretching 343 metres (1,125 feet) above the Tarn River. It also has the highest roadway in the world, at 270 metres (885 feet).

FACTS ✤ Ground-breaking bridges

- 19 BC Pont du Gard **aqueduct**, France. Three-tiered Roman aqueduct.
- AD 610 Great Stone Bridge, China. Early flattened arch.
- 1779 Ironbridge, England. First iron bridge.
- 1849 Britannia Bridge, Wales. First box-**girder** bridge.
- 1874 Eads Bridge, St Louis, USA. First steel bridge.
- 1883 Brooklyn Bridge, New York, USA. First **suspension bridge** with **steel** cables.
- 1884 Garabit Viaduct, France. Early long-**span** iron arch.
- 1890 Forth Railway Bridge, Scotland. First steel **cantilever** bridge.
- 1930 Salginatobel Bridge, Switzerland. Early **reinforced concrete** arch.
- 1931 George Washington Bridge, New York–New Jersey, USA. First very long span   suspension bridge.
- 1956 Stromsund Bridge, Sweden. Early **cable**-stay **bridge**.

Glossary

abutment   support at the end of a bridge

aqueduct   bridge that carries a water channel

arch bridge   bridge supported by one or more arch-shaped structures built end to end

beam   long piece of wood or metal that spans an opening and supports a structure above

beam bridge   bridge made up of a beam supported at its two ends

bearing plate   plate between a beam and a pier that allows the beam to bend and slide slightly

bedrock   hard, solid rock deep underground

borehole   deep, narrow hole bored down into the ground to take samples of the earth and rocks lie below

cable-stay bridge   bridge where the deck is supported from above by cables attached to towers

caisson   large steel or concrete box that is sunk into water and filled with concrete to form a foundation

cantilever   beam supported at just one end

canyon   steep-sided rocky valley

carbon fibre   light, strong material made from fibres of carbon

cement   mixture of materials that hardens into a rock-like substance after it is mixed with water

cofferdam   temporary dam that keeps water from flowing into excavations during construction work

compression   state of being pressed or squashed together

consulting engineer engineer who decides how a structure should be built, rather than an engineer who builds it

contract   become smaller

deck   part of a bridge on which traffic travels

embankment   bank with a flat top and sloping sides

engineer   person who designs or builds a structure

estuary   wide, tidal section of a river, where it meets the sea

expand   get larger

expansion joint   flexible rubber joint between two beams that allows them to expand and contract slightly

foundation   structure that spreads the weight of a bridge and the traffic on it into the ground

geological   to do with the rocks that make up the Earth

girder   beam made of steel plates welded together

gorge   deep, narrow, steep-sided rocky valley

hanger   steel bar or cable that ties a suspension bridge deck to the cable above

in situ   made where it will be used. *In situ* concrete is poured in moulds and sets where it is needed.

kevlar   synthetic (not natural) fibre which is much stronger than steel wire

load   force that presses on a bridge, such as the weight of traffic

pier   vertical support part-way along a bridge

pile   long steel or concrete pole driven deep into the ground

pneumatic   operated by air

pre-cast concrete   concrete that is shaped before it is put in place

prefabricated   made from parts built in a factory

pre-stressed concrete   type of reinforced concrete in which the steel is stretched before concrete is added

reinforced concrete   concrete that contains steel reinforcing bars

silt   very fine soil washed down a river and deposited at its mouth

span   section of a bridge between two supports, the distance between two supports, or the overall length of a bridge

spandrel   vertical support that connects an arch to the road deck held up by the arch

steel   type of very strong metal made mostly of iron

suspension bridge   bridge with a deck that is supported from above by a cable stretched between the ends of the bridge

tension   state of being pulled apart

truss   beam made of a framework of lengths of steel or wood

weld   attach two pieces of metal to each other by heating them until they melt, then joining them together

Index